PIANO | VOCAL | GU...

MICHAEL JAC...

Xscape

ISBN 978-1-4803-9730-9

HAL•LEONARD®
CORPORATION

7777 W. BLUEMOUND RD. P.O. BOX 13819 MILWAUKEE, WI 53213

For all works contained herein:
Unauthorized copying, arranging, adapting, recording, Internet posting, public performance,
or other distribution of the printed music in this publication is an infringement of copyright.

LOVE NEVER FELT SO GOOD

Words and Music by MICHAEL JACKSON
and PAUL ANKA

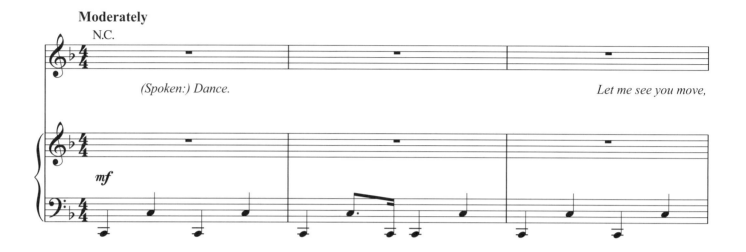

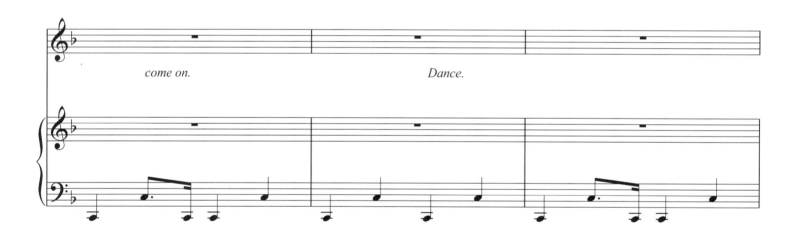

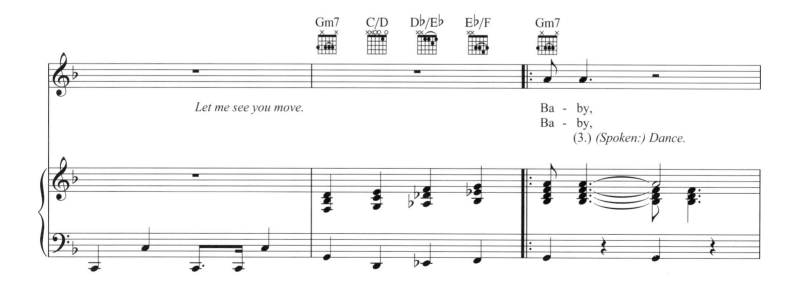

Copyright © 2014 Mijac Music and Paulanne Music Inc.
All Rights on behalf of Mijac Music Administered by Sony/ATV Music Publishing LLC, 424 Church Street, Suite 1200, Nashville, TN 37219
International Copyright Secured   All Rights Reserved

8

CHICAGO

Words and Music by MICHAEL JACKSON
and STEVE PORCARO

Relaxed R&B Groove

Copyright © 2014 Mijac Music and Sony/ATV Tunes LLC
All Rights Administered by Sony/ATV Music Publishing LLC, 424 Church Street, Suite 1200, Nashville, TN 37219
International Copyright Secured   All Rights Reserved

LOVING YOU

Words and Music by
MICHAEL JACKSON

Copyright © 2014 Mijac Music
All Rights Administered by Sony/ATV Music Publishing LLC, 424 Church Street, Suite 1200, Nashville, TN 37219
International Copyright Secured   All Rights Reserved

A PLACE WITH NO NAME

Words and Music by MICHAEL JACKSON,
ELLIOT STRAITE and DEWEY BUNNELL

Lyrics in music:

drove a - cross_ on the high - way,_ my jeep be - gan_ to_ rock.

out, parked the car like side - ways,_ so I can find what I can fix.

I did - n't know what to do, so I stopped

I looked a - round, there were no cars on the high -

Copyright © 2014 Mijac Music, Sony/ATV Songs LLC, Uncle James Music and Warner/Chappell Music Ltd.
All Rights on behalf of Mijac Music, Sony/ATV Songs LLC and Uncle James Music Administered by Sony/ATV Music Publishing LLC, 424 Church Street, Suite 1200, Nashville, TN 37219
All Rights on behalf of Warner/Chappell Music Ltd. in the Western Hemisphere Administered by WB Music Corp.
International Copyright Secured   All Rights Reserved
{Contains Samples of "A Horse With No Name" by Dewey Bunnell, © 1972 (Renewed) Warner/Chappell Music Ltd.}

22

SLAVE TO THE RHYTHM

Words and Music by KENNETH EDMONDS,
DARYL SIMMONS, ANTONIO REID
and KEVIN ROBERSON

Ominously

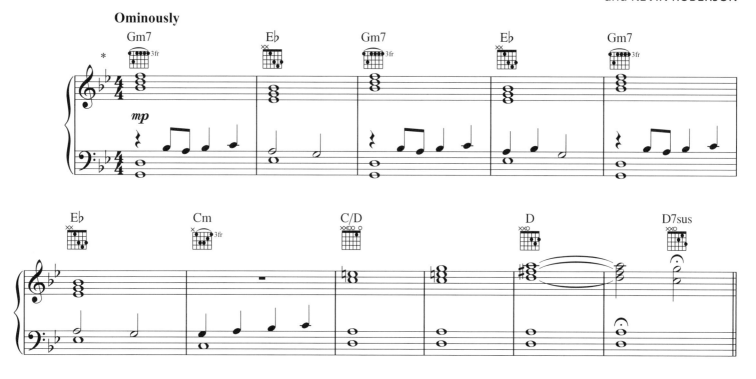

Frenetic Dance Groove

Small notes represent synthesized percussion groove.

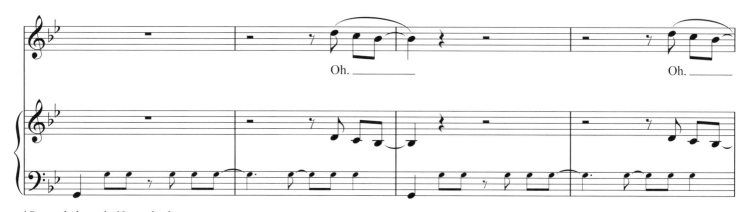

Recorded one half-step higher.

Copyright © 2014 Sony/ATV Songs LLC, Ecaf Music, Warner-Tamerlane Publishing Corp., Boobie And DJ Songs, Inc. and AX5 Songz, LLC
All Rights on behalf of Sony/ATV Songs LLC and Ecaf Music Administered by Sony/ATV Music Publishing LLC, 424 Church Street, Suite 1200, Nashville, TN 37219
All Rights on behalf of Boobie And DJ Songs, Inc. Administered by Warner-Tamerlane Publishing Corp.
International Copyright Secured   All Rights Reserved

DO YOU KNOW WHERE YOUR CHILDREN ARE

Words and Music by
MICHAEL JACKSON

Copyright © 2014 Mijac Music
All Rights Administered by Sony/ATV Music Publishing LLC, 424 Church Street, SUite 1200, Nashville, TN 37219
International Copyright Secured All Rights Reserved

BLUE GANGSTA

Words and Music by MICHAEL JACKSON
and ELLIOT STRAITE

Copyright © 2014 Mijac Music, Sony/ATV Songs LLC and Uncle James Music
All Rights Administered by Sony/ATV Music Publishing LLC, 424 Church Street, Suite 1200, Nashville, TN 37219
International Copyright Secured   All Rights Reserved

XSCAPE

Words and Music by MICHAEL JACKSON,
LASHAWN DANIELS, RODNEY JERKINS
and FRED JERKINS

Rhythmic Pop groove

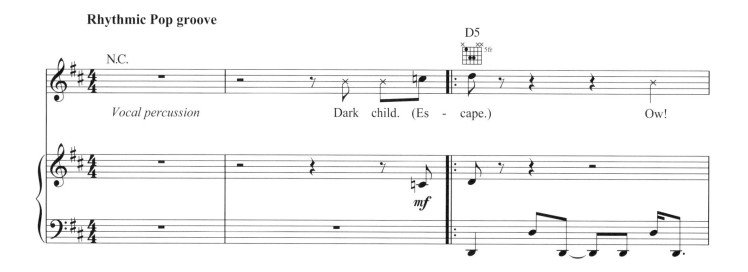

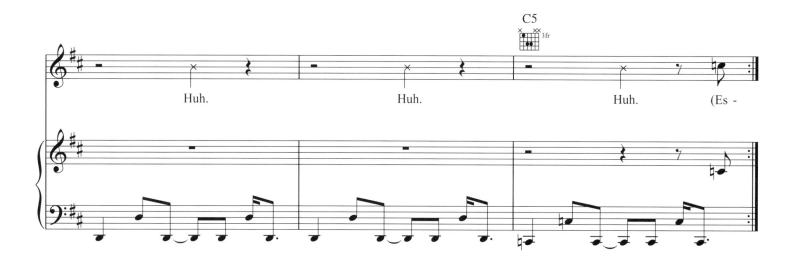

Copyright © 2014 Mijac Music, EMI April Music Inc., The Book Productions LLC, Rodney Jerkins Productions Inc. and Fred Jerkins Publishing
All Rights on behalf of Mijac Music, EMI April Music Inc. and The Book Productions LLC Administered by Sony/ATV Music Publishing LLC, 424 Church Street, Suite 1200, Nashville, TN 37219
All Rights on behalf of Rodney Jerkins Productions Inc. Administered by BMG Rights Management (US) LLC
International Copyright Secured   All Rights Reserved